WHEN PIGS FLY

**Winner of 2nd Place Award
in the Writing for Children category,
Writers' Federation of New Brunswick, 2007.**

"... a splendid collection of poetry that captures the concerns and experiences of childhood, then puts a wild and wacky twist on each of them. There are unexpected delights on every page because this poet knows exactly how to begin and end a rhyme, and always manages to surprise the reader. And the bouncing, galloping rhymes consistently play games with the reader and tickle all the senses. Children will giggle over these poems, as will the adults who are sharing them."

— from the judge's comments

When Pigs Fly
& Other Poems

BY
MICHELLE MCLEAN

ILLUSTRATIONS BY
SOPHIE ARSENEAU

CHAPEL STREET KIDS

© 2020 Michelle McLean
All rights reserved

Published by
Chapel Street Editions
150 Chapel Street
Woodstock, New Brunswick E7M 1H4
www.chapelstreeteditions.com

ISBN 978-1-988299-29-7

Library and Archives Canada Cataloguing in Publication

Title: When pigs fly & other poems / by Michelle McLean ;
    illustrations by Sophie Arseneau.
Other titles: When pigs fly and other poems
Names: McLean, Michelle, 1975- author. | Arseneau, Sophie, 2007- illustrator.
Identifiers: Canadiana 20200276913 | ISBN 9781988299297 (softcover)
Classification: LCC PS8625.L4293 W54 2020 | DDC jC811/.6—dc23

All illustrations by Sophie Arseneau except for
"Kindred" on page 56 by Lily Arseneau.

Book design by Brendan Helmuth

Dedication

For my daughters, Sophie and Lily,
who make everything worth it.

And for my mother,
who always leaves the light on for me.

CONTENTS

Introduction 1
  When Pigs Fly 2
  Something Dreadful Has Happened 4
  Food Fight 5
  Nude Ranch 6
  There's an Apple in My Worm 7
  Snug as a Bug 8
  There's a Kitty in This Sandbox 9
  Bravado 10
  The Complainer 11
  Prolific 12
  Slip of the Tongue. 13
    Almost Perfect 14
      Homeward Bound 15
      What's the Matter Weeping Willow? 16
      Perspective 17
      Who Has Broken the Wind? 18
    Dreamsicle 19
  Simon McGrue. 20
  Opportunist 21
  The Pot and the Kettle. 22
  Sisters 23
  Karma. 24
  Delia Divine 25
  Dream On 26

Tall Tail?	28
Mitsy's Bed	29
Afterthought	30
Life at Three	31
Brainfood?	32
Beware the Frumps	33
Greedy Gretchen	34
Deadbeat Daisy	35
Architect Advice	36
The Beach	37
Finger, The Explorer	38
Biff McSnood	39
Sighers	40
It's Raining in Our Kitchen	41
Vantage Point	42
Jane Indignant	43
I Have an Itchy Heart	45
The Swargle	46
Wardrobe Malfunction	47
Adaptation	48
Cruel Chef	49
Clotheslion	50
Piggy Bank	51
Ms. Woebegone	52
Fingernails	53
Misanthrope	54
Diplomat	55

Kindred	56
Boomerang Blues	57
A Costly Bath	58
Marvin Ate the Moon	59
Lucky Penny	60
Road Rage?	61
I Had a Spurt of Growth	62
Bookworming	63
Appearance vs. Reality	64
Says Who?	65
The Song In Me	66
Einstein's Hair	67
The Boogeyman	68
Crocus Pocus	69
The Lesson	70
Dragonflies	71
Sad Gruffy	72
Gesundheit	74
Clairvoyant Clara	76
The Musician	77
In the Company of Clouds	78
Acknowledgments	81
About the Author	83
About the Illustrator	83

INTRODUCTION

While conceived years prior, *When Pigs Fly* really took shape as a collection when my eldest child — and the book's illustrator — was in utero.

When Pigs Fly was awarded second place in the Writer's Federation of New Brunswick's annual contest in the "Writing for Children" category (2007); collaborating on this project with my daughter has made publication well worth the wait.

I think my favorite description of this collection came from my publisher, who called it "delightfully quirky" — an observation consistent with my vision of creating a joyful blend of whimsy, warmth, and playful, goofy fun. We hope you have a "delightfully quirky" time with these poems!

– Michelle McLean

WHEN PIGS FLY

Pigs are flying overhead;
it really blows my mind!
A monstrous sow is in the front
with hundreds close behind.

They're wearing no propellers,
no balloons around their waist
and it kind of makes me wonder
how would all THIS bacon taste?

SOMETHING DREADFUL HAS HAPPENED

Something dreadful has happened –
I think I may have a disease!
It's given me much trepidation
and a frightful sense of unease.

I guess I should go to the doctor;
I'm plagued from my neck to my knees!
I know I'm a little bit chilly
but what kind of goosebumps are THESE?

FOOD FIGHT

It's hard to say who started
this refrigerator brawl
but once the thing got started
it became a free-for-all!

The ketchup slapped the mustard
and the mayo tripped the cheese;
the chocolate milk got lippy
with the cold, leftover peas.

The pickles pinched the potroast
and the eggs demeaned the fruit.
The orange juice objected
and the carrots followed suit.

Soon everyone was shouting—
they were causing quite a buzz!
Till someone caught a glimpse
of the incandescent fuzz.

No one knew what it had been
in the life it had before
but once it started MOVING
they weren't fighting anymore!

NUDE RANCH

I came for the job on your nude ranch;
I ran just as fast as I could.
I always wanted to work on a nude ranch –
but perhaps I have misunderstood?

THERE'S AN APPLE IN MY WORM

I really must object
to this apple in my worm
for it isn't what I ordered
and besides, it doesn't squirm.

I hate to be a bother;
I am loathe to say a word
but dining can be picky
when you're eating like a bird.

SNUG AS A BUG

Just how snug is a bug in a rug?
Let's ask this one to see –
he's awfully quiet, lying there.
I think you will agree
that bugs in rugs are pretty snug
and really kind of sweet.
Rugs are snug
for little bugs
if people watch their feet.

THERE'S A KITTY IN THIS SANDBOX

There's a kitty in this sandbox —
all you children best beware.
There's a kitty in this sandbox,
in the center, nestled there.

> There's a kitty in this sandbox;
> when you're playing, please take care —
>
> > though she's not very big,
> > just watch out where you dig —
> >
> > > a surprise might be buried in there...

BRAVADO

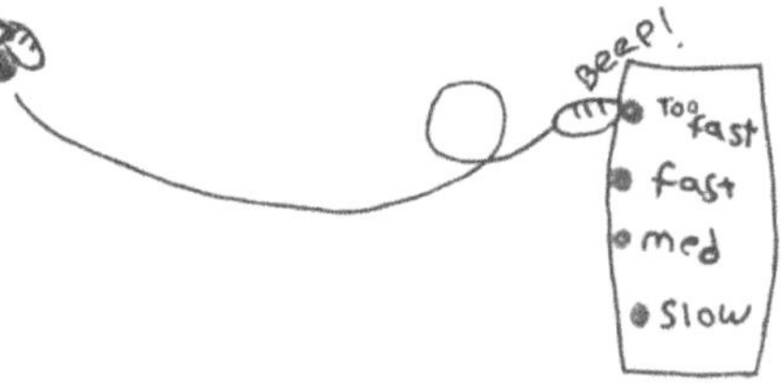

Foolish Fran rode the ceiling fan
by hanging on with her teeth.

Someone turned up the speed
but she didn't take heed
and that's why this story's so brief.

THE COMPLAINER

The butter's too hard;
the soup is too cold.
My mom is too strict
and dad is too old.

The day is too cloudy;
my swimsuit's too wet.
I'm fed up with watching
this small T.V. set.

The house is too drafty;
the kitchen's too small.
This book is too short
and its tale is too tall.

This pencil's too sharp;
this crossword's too tricky.
You are too patient
and I am too picky.

PROLIFIC

These amorous rabbits
have troublesome habits
of making such work for Lenore!

Gadzooks, what to do?
They've produced eighty-two
and each month
there's a dozenish more.

SLIP OF THE TONGUE

It's hard some days for a tongue;
I'm forced to eat what I'm fed
and I never get the credit
for anything I've said.

I don't much like complaining
and I really hate to pout
but sometimes when I'm really mad
you'll find me sticking out.

ALMOST PERFECT

If you are seeking to impress,
you'll have to move with more finesse.
Your limbs are gangly—much too long.
You're also bold and too headstrong.

I guess I must be truthful, here—
your fashion sense is rather queer;
that scarf is like a funeral shroud
and really, must you laugh so loud?

You never let me win at chess;
it's quite off-putting, I confess.
You bite your nails and scuff your feet.
Your tax returns are incomplete.

You think too much. I don't know why
your face gets puffy when you cry.
Your hairstyle needs an overhaul
(I also find your nose too small).

And now I see your temper's short
(I never dreamed you were THAT sort)
aside from that, I think you're fine—
now won't you be my Valentine?

HOMEWARD BOUND

I am an intrepid, nomadic snail –
the house on my back is so great!
I have a home wherever I roam
but it's hard to renovate…

WHAT'S THE MATTER WEEPING WILLOW?

What's the matter weeping willow?
Why are you so glum?
Why aren't your branches growing
to the sky and toward the sun?
I'm really quite enamored with
the leaves in which you're clad;
what's the matter weeping willow—
why are you so sad?

PERSPECTIVE

Randal Lafiti likes graffiti –
he's always painting the town.
Some people call him genius
but others chase him down.

WHO HAS BROKEN THE WIND?

I thought I had my Bum
all neatly packed away
and though the time was wrong,
Bum had its piece to say.

It quickly cleared the room
much to my grave dismay.
I've been so mad at Bum
since it farted in ballet!

DREAMSICLE

Penny had a dreamsicle,
a sweet and bright delight
but she didn't want to eat it
till she felt the time was right.

    So she held on to it tightly
    with its future in her hands
    but why she wouldn't take a bite
    nobody understands.

        She measured for its size
        and weighed it pound for pound
        but soon that droopy dreamsicle
        was a puddle on the ground.

SIMON MCGRUE

Simon McGrue was playing with glue,
happy as can be.

I laughed and I teased
but I'm not really pleased

'cause now he's sticking to me.

OPPORTUNIST

Flies
with wise eyes
settle on pies.

THE POT AND THE KETTLE

While I was sitting in the kitchen
Pot and Kettle had a fight
and no matter what was said,
each insisted he was right.

Soon Pot flew off the handle
and Kettle blew his top
but they both became quite silent
once the OVEN hollered STOP!

SISTERS

I have a little sister
who follows me around
and when I'm playing hide (not seek!)
I find I'm always found.

She's a dragon-slaying
mischief-making
pain in my behind.
She's loud and rough but fiercely fun,
exuberant and kind.

She makes faces at the table
and she crawls upon the floor.
She makes my blood go boiling
like it's never boiled before!

She likes to give me presents
which she wraps with style and flair
and when I'm hurt or scared or sad,
my sister's always there.

Inventing games and stories,
running kingdoms, big and small;
imagination guides our world—
we laugh and have a ball.

We wrestle and we wrangle
and we sometimes fuss and fight
but she's still my little sister
who I love with all my might.

KARMA

There's few things more delightful
than a picnic in the park;
I often go at noontime
and stay till almost dark.

And it only stands to reason,
pick up your trash when you're through
or the birds that call this park their home
may decide to "litter" on YOU!

DELIA DIVINE

I'm Delia Divine, my clothes are fine
and I am perfect all the time.

I do not scowl; I will not spit.
I do not poke; I never hit.
I do not eat before I dine;
when bedtime comes, I never whine.

I don't like speaking out of turn.
I'm never cause for much concern.
I do not shout, nor do I sing;
I don't do much of anything.

I'm Delia Divine–I'm so refined
and I am perfect all the time.

DREAM ON

My mind is playing hide and seek
through the meadow, across the creek
past where the willows bend and sway
beneath the softly dappled day.

   If you should find it out, today,
   kindly send it back my way.
   Please ensure its safe return;
   my mind has yet a lot to learn.

      I'm watching fields of flowers blow;
      my mind's still hiding, but I know
      that I will find it sometime soon
      (I need it back this afternoon!)

         But at this time, my impish mind
         has left the rest of me behind.
         It needs to roam; it cannot rest
         to focus on this standard test.

My mind was never meant for small;
it gathers stories, short and tall.
My mind has deeper work, you know
while seeking to align its flow.

I sit and smile and watch it grow.

TALL TAIL?

My kitty's tail is a million feet high;
it waves at the clouds and tickles the sky.
I don't know how and no one knows why
but look at this face—do you think I would lie?

MITSY'S BED

Mitsy just can't sleep without
her toys tucked in her bed –
her pretty purple elephant,
her dog, and Mr. Zed.

Her dollies are all nestled
in a shiny cargo train
with no consideration
for the growing mattress strain.

She brings to bed her ponies,
her drums and xylophone;
Mitsy's never been a fan
of sleeping all alone.

She's brought her new computer,
some trinkets, trucks and more.
There's now no space for Mitsy
so she sleeps upon the floor.

AFTERTHOUGHT

Mouth and Brain had a race
to determine the saving of face.

Mouth promptly won.
Now, what's to be done?

Poor Brain needs to pick up the pace!

LIFE AT THREE

My bloomers are starting to bloom
like they've never bloomed before
as I cautiously circle the room
and try to look demure.

I'll grant you that it's strange,
but it's nothing to condemn.
My bloomers are starting to bloom
because I've watered them.

BRAINFOOD?

I eat fish every day.
They say it's good for your brain.
I give them plenty of water
'cause I like to be humane.

BEWARE THE FRUMPS

Beware the frumps
who criticize,
the grumps who scowl
with beady eyes.

It should come as no surprise—
the chumps can't tell
the truth from lies.

And from these frumps
and grumps and chumps,
beware of taking any lumps.

GREEDY GRETCHEN

You could say I have a sweet tooth,
a most healthy appetite.
Some might say, "that's too much sugar";
I'd be apt to say "Just right!"

So when Nana baked a cake
scrumptious looking as could be,
I cut myself a serving
while my Nan prepared the tea.

She said "My dear, that's rather selfish
and it isn't very nice."
I don't know what she's mad about –
I only took one slice!

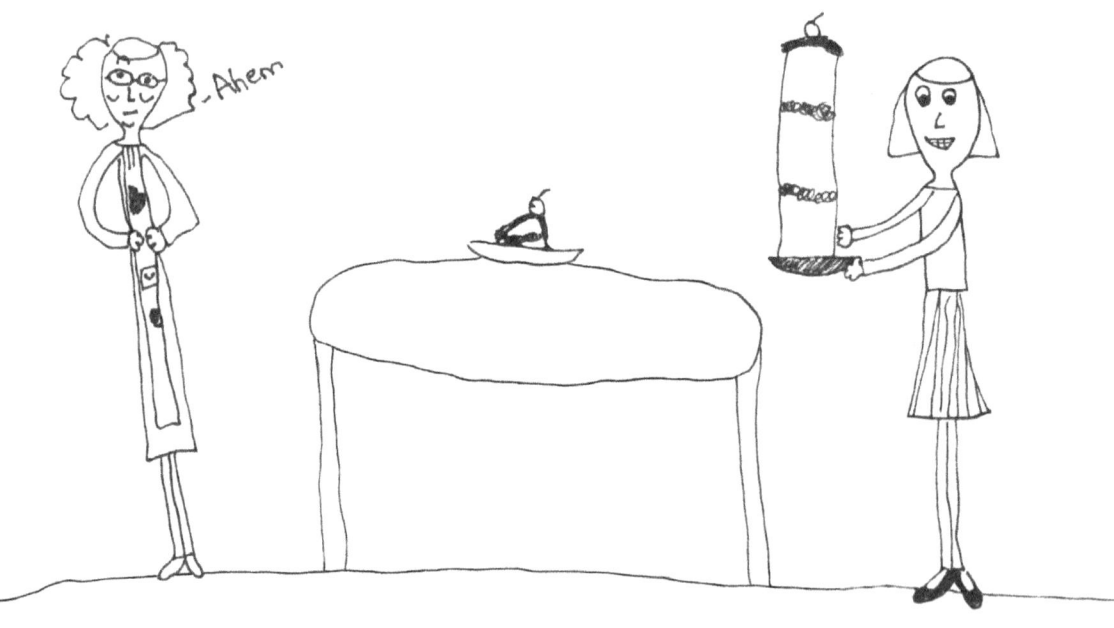

DEADBEAT DAISY

This petal claims he loves me
but this one says no way;
my third pick is a winner but
the next response is "nay".

I've lost track of the answer
after plucking all of them.
So now I sit here wondering
holding nothing but the stem.

ARCHITECT ADVICE

Now, before we build this snow fort,
there's something you should know—
when it's time to break for lunch,
you mustn't eat the yellow snow!

THE BEACH

Nothing beats a summer day,
with ocean surf just yards away.

I smile at all the folks I meet
wandering aimless, bare of feet.

The sand is hot, but the water's not.
You don't need a mansion; you don't need a yacht.

The best things in life
are most certainly free
when the waves of the ocean
are waving at me.

FINGER, THE EXPLORER

Finger, the explorer
is off to parts unknown
taking with him dreams of treasure
and the hand he calls his home.

He didn't take a suitcase
and he didn't take a map;
that's all well and good
but what is Finger bringing BACK?

BIFF MCSNOOD

My name is Biff McSnood
and I'm intolerably rude —
invite me to your dinner table
and I'll insult the food.

I'll cut in line most anytime
and never wait my turn.
I'll butt my nose in anything
that's far from my concern.

I'll interrupt your dialogue
and spit upon your floor.
No one asks me for my thoughts
or opinions anymore.

For despite my other attributes
you simply must conclude
that I, Biff McSnood,
am intolerably rude.

SIGHERS

Sighs are flying,
sighs are sinking –
what are all the sighers thinking?

Thoughts content
of time well spent?

Or thoughts of sadness
and lament?

Do they sigh for lemondrops
and lovely, luscious lollipops?

Perhaps they're sighs of great frustration

    or is it merely contemplation?

If I sigh when passing by

    will you stop and ask me why?

IT'S RAINING IN OUR KITCHEN

It's raining in our kitchen –
there are buckets everywhere.
If you're needing any water,
there's ample here to spare.

It's raining in our kitchen –
awfully strange, but it's the truth.
It's raining in our kitchen
ever since Dad fixed the roof.

VANTAGE POINT

"I hate my job," Toothbrush cried.
"Back and forth, side to side
cleaning foul mouths night and day
with barely time to rest or play."

"You think that's bad?" Kleenex said.
"Why not take MY job instead?
Crumpled up and cast aside,
tossed in trash cans far and wide."

Toilet flushed without a word,
sick of all the gripes he'd heard.
The others blushed and looked away
with nothing, really, left to say.

JANE INDIGNANT

Jane Indignant in a rage
is like a tiger in a cage.
If you dare to flip this page
she looks like...

THIS...!

-AHHHH!

I HAVE AN ITCHY HEART

I have an itchy heart
and I'm feeling mighty blue.
I guess that I can't scratch it
so I don't know what I'll do.

It's quite an odd sensation
but trust me that it's true.
I have an itchy heart
because I'm really missing you.

THE SWARGLE

I am the Swargle—
I likes to gargle;
I drives the swimmers to fits.
If you're in the lake when I takes me a drink,
you'd better hopes I spits!

WARDROBE MALFUNCTION

My throat is dry.
My head is light.

My face is red.
My ears are white.

Something surely isn't right—
perhaps my tie's a tad too tight!

ADAPTATION

My kitty can't play in our band
for she has no opposable thumbs.
She can't play the tuba or keyboard,
not bass guitar nor drums.

Poor kitty can't play the cymbals
and certainly nothing that strums.
Although she plays no instrument,
she expertly purrs and hums.

CRUEL CHEF

I beat the eggs;
I whipped the batter.
I pounded the dough
to make it flatter.

I greased the pan;
I shredded the cheese.
I rolled up the mixture
and left it to freeze.

I fried the fish
and hacked off its tail;
perhaps it's time
you sent me to jail.

CLOTHESLION

My laundry's been through a disaster.
My pants are shredded clear through!
My socks are nothing but holes and
my bed sheets are all mangled too.

My sewing can't salvage my wardrobe.
I don't know what I can do.
I suppose this hungry old clotheslion
will have to return to the zoo.

PIGGY BANK

Our excursion to the Piggy Bank
was sheer catastrophe –
the tellers kept eating the money
and charged us a processing fee.

They snorted in response
when we asked them for a loan
and took complete control
over everything we own.

As they gobbled up our savings
leaving us without a shred
we started to object
"It's collateral", they said.

They buried us in forms
as they munched their way along
but since they're such a Piggy Bank
it's not where we belong.

MS. WOEBEGONE

Ms. Woebegone happened upon
a mangled little dream;
she picked it up, took it home
and stitched it at the seam.

She gave it love and sunshine
and nursed it till it grew.
And soon that mangled little dream
was looking good as new.

FINGERNAILS

There are nails growing out of my fingers;
when I type, they make such a clamor!
I cannot clip them, neat and trim –
I have to use a hammer.

MISANTHROPE

He's growlish and grumpish
and meanish and lumpish,
this glowering, grumbling, miserable man.

He's easily irked
and his staff's overworked;
he'll insult you with vigor whenever he can.

He's peevish and snarlish
unkindish and gnarlish;
he's rude to your face and worse on the phone.

It's odd, I have found,
he wants no one around
but there's nothing he hates more than being alone.

DIPLOMAT

My bowl and my plate
had a bitter debate
over whom was best to use,
so I served up soup and sandwiches
and no one had to lose.

KINDRED

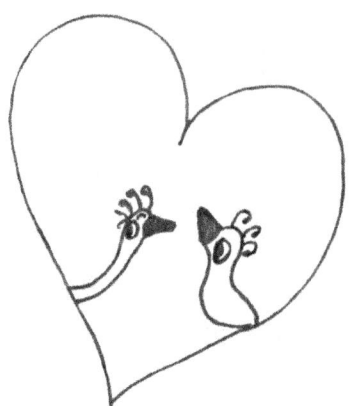

Birds of a feather flock together,
at least that's what they say.
I'm fond of your feathers
in all kinds of weathers –
will you come out and play?

I'm fond of your stories. I'm fond of your songs.
I love your magnificent voice!
Your eyes, how they shine,
your plumage, divine;
hands down, you're my number one choice.

Birds of a feather, that's what we are –
a duo dynamic, it's true.
No matter wherever
we're better together;
my happiest me is with you.

BOOMERANG BLUES

I have a need for speed
and I love a change of scene.
I like to catch a break
from the tired, old routine.

I try to see the world
but it gets me rather glum
'cause no matter where I go,
I come back to where I'm from.

A COSTLY BATH

My hands are all in a flurry
scrubbing my belly and face.
My legs are terrifically soapy;
there's water all over the place.

Bubbles and sudsies galore
have settled themselves in my hair.
My clothes are drenched clear through
from my shirt to my underwear.

My mother says "You're grounded!"
but my dad can only frown.
No more can I go to the car wash
since I left the windows down.

MARVIN ATE THE MOON

He heard it was made of cheese
so Marvin ate the moon;
he golloped up the whole darn thing
with a sparkling silver spoon.

And though it may sound strange,
I guess it's true, they say –
Marvin brought along his cup
and drank up the milky way!

LUCKY PENNY

A black cat crossed my path
and mama let me keep it.
I broke the hallway mirror
but I didn't have to sweep it.

I walked beneath a ladder
and found a ten dollar bill.
I ran up thirteen steps
and never took a spill.

I guess I'm pretty lucky;
what else am I to say?
I really don't know why—
was I simply born this way?

ROAD RAGE?

They told me to hit the road
so I got me a shovel and spike,
a sledgehammer, stick and a pickaxe,
a flyswatter, mallet and pipe.
I worked myself into a road rage
and whacked the road with aplomb,
but now I'm feeling guilty-
the road has done nothing wrong!

I HAD A SPURT OF GROWTH

I had a spurt of growth
and I think my clothes have shrunk.
I always wanted to be taller
but now I'm in a funk.

They say I'll stop this growing
but I hope it's pretty soon—
I went to bed at four feet ten
and woke up on the moon!

BOOKWORMING

I was quietly reading my book
when the characters dragged me inside;
so now that I'm here in the plot,
I guess I'm along for the ride.

I'm stuck in the thick of the action
and nothing can bring me back out;
I can't even answer the phone
or my mother's supper shout.

There's all kinds of intrigue and drama
and battles both lost and won.
I'm stuck in their cliffhanger clutches
till the final chapter is done.

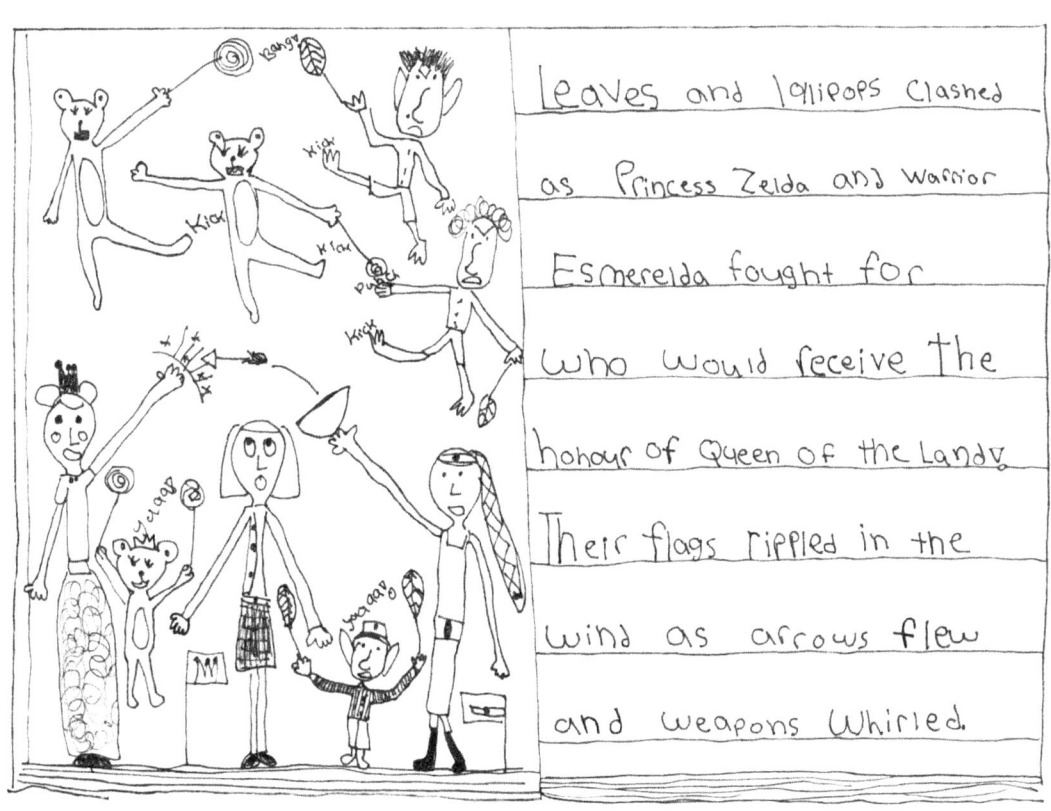

Leaves and lollipops clashed as Princess Zelda and warrior Esmerelda fought for who would receive the honour of Queen of the Land. Their flags rippled in the wind as arrows flew and weapons whirled.

APPEARANCE VS. REALITY

Resplendent like the morning dew,
you glide with grace and class;
you're smooth and svelte and elegant
but you're still a snake in the grass!

SAYS WHO?

"You're different and odd"
this chap used to say
"I mean, who has a nose for an ear?"

It's better, I say,
any time, any day,

than having a head for a rear!

THE SONG IN ME

My father loves his baseball
but me, I love to dance.
He can't seem to appreciate
the skill with which I prance.

I begged for ballet lessons
but got a mitt instead,
so I joined the baseball team
with Tchaikovsky in my head.

When my bat first cracked the ball
I knew that I was set,
so I celebrated at first base
with a perfect pirouette.

My father sat there watching
but he didn't say a word
as I twirled my way to second base
and plied into third.

The crowd all seemed to love it
but my dad could only groan
as I kicked my heels up in the air
and fluttered into home.

I have to be myself
and I guess it's plain to see that
I just can't keep from dancing
with these songs inside of me.

EINSTEIN'S HAIR

Einstein's hair is long and fair;
it's debonair beyond compare.
He wears it with such style and flair;
it grows an inch a day, I swear.

Do not braid it—please forebear!
He likes to keep it laissez-faire.

Whenever you see Einstein's hair
do try not to stare…

THE BOOGEYMAN

Some folks call me the boogeyman.
I don't mean to give you a fright.
I sleep all day in my hideaway
'cause I likes to boogey all night!

CROCUS POCUS

Some people think it's magic
when I appear on the scene.
My friends all wait till springtime
when the world is turning green.

Perhaps I'm overeager,
it's quite chilly out, I know –
but crocus pocus, here I come,
blooming through the snow!

THE LESSON

There's oozy bruisy marks
on my puckered, peppered face
and I'm stinging in my back and arms,
my knees, and every place.

I know I've lost some blood
and a fever's sure to come.
I'll be surprised if I don't DIE
before this day is done.

"Ya takes your knocks", my brother said
"It doesn't help to whine.
You might have known it's ill-advised
to hug a porcupine!"

DRAGONFLIES

These dragonflies that fill the skies
are something to admire

but you'd better keep your distance
when you see them breathing fire!

SAD GRUFFY

I cannot flee from the flea
who's sitting, now, on my knee
for he seems to prefer to crawl through my fur
without apology.

A most compelling plea
I shared with him over tea;
I said, "Please don't grieve, but you really must leave."
Though on this we still disagree.

I'm tough and strong as can be;
he's half the size of a pea
but my bristling brawn just inspires a yawn
for he's loathe to listen to me.

I've been on a scratching spree
since he's joined my company!
I suppose I could eat him
if I could just reach him
and end this misery.

I fear I'll never be free
of the beast I carry with me.
He's really a pest, but tenacious, I guess
for I cannot flee from the flea.

GESUNDHEIT

I couldn't stop sneezing all weekend.
My parents can testify
this sneezing has lifted me off of my feet
and carried me up to the sky.

My sneeze, it took me to China;
I danced on the Great Wall there.
I achooed my way to Mozambique
then on to Delaware.

I sneezed myself to Singapore
then all the way to France;
a sneeze flew me to Holland
where I watched the tulips dance.

I sneezed my way through Canada—
a wonder to behold.
But now I'm done with traveling
for I seem to be over my cold.

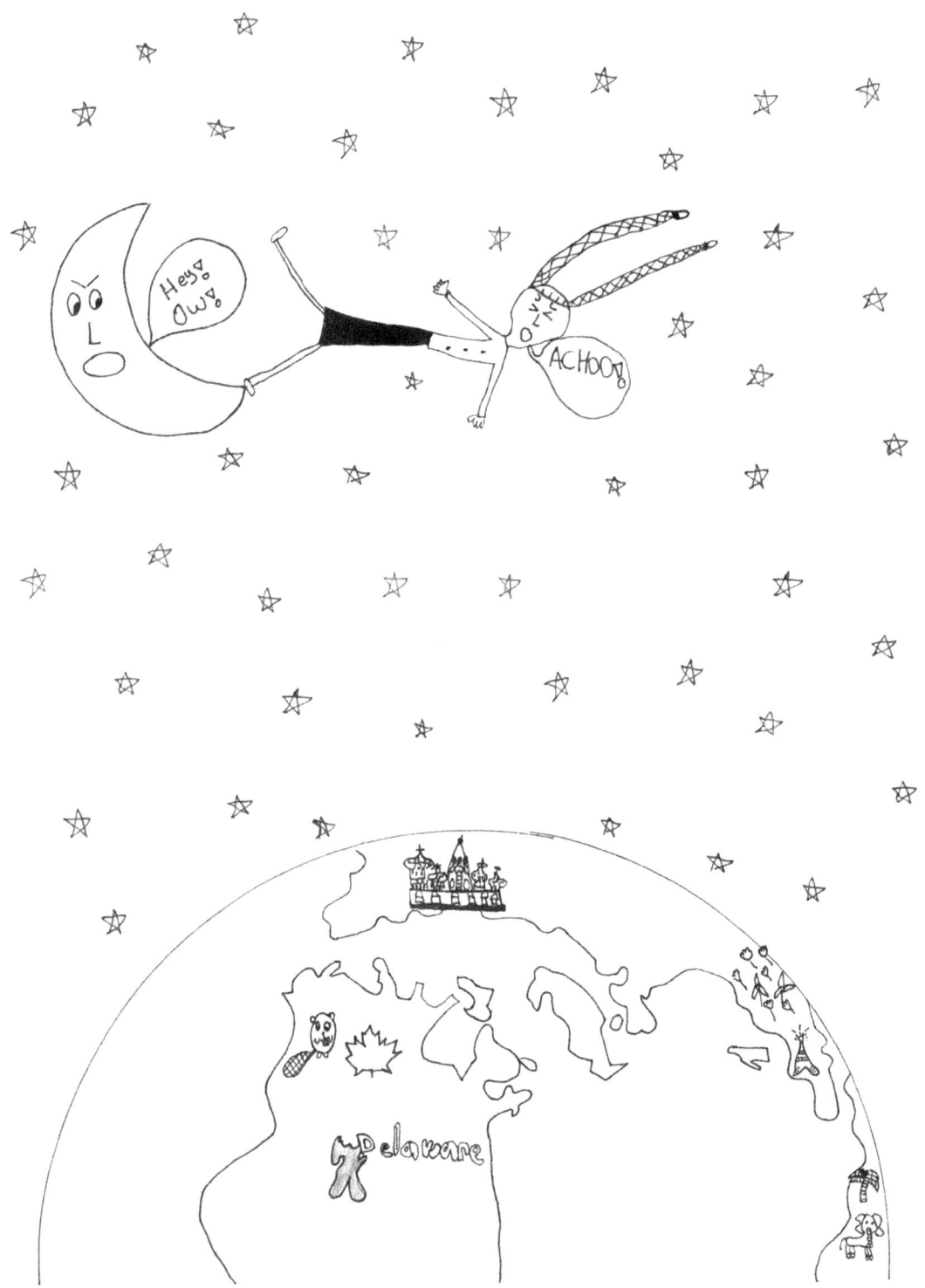

CLAIRVOYANT CLARA

The name's clairvoyant Clara.
I've the gift of second sight.
Is it going to rain, you ask?
It may. It could. It might...

I sense impending danger
if you ride atop your car
and I feel that where you go
will soon be where you are.

The name's Clairvoyant Clara—
for your fortune I will tell
all the future you can ask
and all that I can sell.

But you say you have no money?
Well, I really must confide—
I said I tell the future
but I'm afraid I lied.

THE MUSICIAN

I once knew a rockin' guitarist —
an awfully talented bloke

but he spent all his money on a harpsichord
and now he's completely baroque.

IN THE COMPANY OF CLOUDS

In the company of clouds
I whisper secrets to the sky
with a Mona Lisa smile
for all the people passing by.

The clouds are ambling through the air
floating fabulously free –
kind of like the dreamings
of a dreaming girl like me.

In the company of clouds
I hear my spirit softly sing
and I cannot help but feel
that I can do most anything.

ACKNOWLEDGMENTS

I am deeply grateful to my daughter, Sophie Arseneau, for her talent, hard work and perseverance in creating the illustrations for this book. It was an ambitious project for an 10/11-year-old to take on, and I am tremendously proud of her. Special thanks as well to my youngest daughter, Lily Arseneau, for her beautiful illustration of "Kindred"; I am thrilled to have her contribution included in this collection.

Warm gratitude to Keith, Ellen, and Brendan Helmuth at Chapel Street Editions for believing in our project and giving it a voice. Thanks to Brigitte Rivers for her artistic guidance and to Paul Twyford for promoting and showcasing Sophie's artwork in Creek Village Gallery's Young Artist Spotlight. Thanks to Greg MacPherson for his generous funding of the Young Artists program, an exciting and confidence-building opportunity for the youth in our community.

Many thanks to the Writer's Federation of New Brunswick and the Odd Sundays crew for their encouragement and support. Thanks to Kathy Mac, Sherry Coffey and David Watts for inviting me as a featured reader in the Odd Sundays series. Warm gratitude to Jenn Carson, Roger Moore, Bryn Harris, Inbal Bahar and Wanda MacFarlane for their friendship, feedback, and encouragement.

Thanks to so many other wonderful folks in our writing community, too numerous to count. Special thanks to Sheree Fitch for taking the time to review our project and for her generous words of praise. Boundless thanks to my

cousin, sounding-board and kindred spirit, Kayte McLaughlin, for inspiriting my "coming out" as a writer, and for being the first reader of this collection so many years ago. Thanks to my partner, James Arseneau, for readily supplying bedside coffee during editing sessions. Love and thanks to friends and family near and far, for your nurturing, enthusiasm, kindness, support, and laughter. Deepest gratitude to my mother, Heather McLean, for keeping me well-supplied with books from a tender age, and for her unwavering faith in me. And finally, thank YOU, dear readers, for holding this book in your hands, recommending it to your friends (yes, please!) and for gifting our work with your time and attention.
We hope you enjoy it!

ABOUT THE AUTHOR

Michelle McLean is a clinical social worker, educator, award-winning poet, and mother of two fabulous, big-hearted daughters. Her work has appeared in a variety of publications, including *Quills, Ascent Aspirations, Understorey, Other Voices, Peacock Journal, JONAH*, and others. She lives with her family in the village of Bath, New Brunswick.

ABOUT THE ILLUSTRATOR

Sophie Arseneau, now 12, completed the illustrations for this collection between the ages of 10-11. Sophie is an artist, writer, and competitive dancer.

www.ingramcontent.com/pod-product-compliance
Lightning Source LLC
Chambersburg PA
CBHW081405070526
44583CB00020B/2686